Pirates

Contents

Villains of the Sea	2
Pirate Ships	6
Pirate Treasure	12
Pirate Flags	16
A Pirate Attack	18
Pirates of the Caribbean	20
Famous Pirates	22
Interesting Pirate Stories	30
Glossary	32

Written by Brian Roberts

Villains of the Sea

It is much safer to travel by sea today than it was hundreds of years ago. Then, there was a very real risk of being attacked and even killed by pirates, privateers, or buccaneers looking for treasure, medicine, or food to steal.

Pirates

Pirates were the *robbers of the sea*. They attacked ships at sea and stole the cargo. Sometimes they anchored their ships on the coast and attacked settlements. The pirates kept anything they stole for themselves.

Many pirates were criminals who killed their victims. Some were just men who wanted to earn much more than they could as sailors or farm workers. Pirates could become very rich from the treasure they stole.

Privateers

Privateers were paid by the government of a country to attack the ships of another country when they were at war.

Privateers shared the riches they took off the ships with the government that had hired them.

Often privateers became pirates because they could make more money that way. When peace treaties were signed between countries, the pirates claimed that the treaties did not apply to them. They kept attacking ships anyway.

Pirates were criminals who attacked, and even killed, their victims.

Buccaneers

Buccaneers were privateers who were no longer paid by their government after peace treaties had been signed. Buccaneers then began attacking ships on their own. They thought that they were better than pirates.

But really, there was little difference between pirates, privateers, and buccaneers. It was difficult to tell one from another.

Pirate Ships

Pirates learned that small, fast ships were best for attacking large, slow, cargo ships. Ships built by governments for privateers were some of the best ships on the seas.

Galleys

Greek pirates that sailed in the Mediterranean Sea over 1,500 years ago used smaller ships called galleys. Galleys had a single mast and were powered by oars and sails.

Chinese Junks

Chinese junks were common pirate ships, built and used in the Far East by the Chinese. Chinese junks carried large crews and could hold more than 25 cannons.

Pirogues

The early buccaneers who lived on the Caribbean islands used boats called pirogues that were carved out of large tree trunks.

Pirogues had small sails and oars for power. It was hard to see them sneaking up on big ships.

Single-Mast Sloops

Single-mast sloops were very fast ships used by pirates in the Caribbean Sea. They were much smaller than galleys or Chinese junks, and they were fast so they could overcome bigger, slower, cargo ships.

The Adventure Galley

One of the most famous pirate ships was the *Adventure Galley*. It was built in London, England, and captained by Captain Kidd, a pirate who had been a privateer.

The main source of power for the ship was the wind, and the *Adventure Galley* had three large masts to hold its mainsails.

The *Adventure Galley* was also equipped with oars to power the ship when there was no wind. The ship held a crew of nearly 125 men.

Pirate Treasure

Pirates robbed ships for the valuable treasure that they carried. Cargoes of gold, silver, gems, silk, sugar, tobacco, and spices were the most valued. The gold and silver might be in the form of coins, plates, goblets, or even church valuables.

However, the pirates also robbed the ships of medicines and food.

Spain set up colonies along the coast in Latin and South America. Spanish soldiers would trade and steal gold, silver, spices, and other valuables from the natives. They would ship the valuable cargo back to Spain in large ships. These ships were targets for many pirates.

A ship carrying valuable cago is attacked by pirate ship

After a raid, the pirates would go off and divide the treasure among themselves. The amount each crew member got was usually decided before they joined a ship. The captain received a double share, crew got an equal share, and the cabin boys got a half share.

Despite many stories about buried pirate treasure, very little has ever been found. Most treasure has come from sunken ships.

There are many stories about pirate treasure.

Richest Pirate Treasure
(based on value of pounds in 1600–1700)

Year	Captain	Value (in pounds sterling)
1579	Francis Drake	450,000
1585	Richard Greenville	50,000
1587	Tom Cavendish	125,000
1587	Francis Drake	114,000
1591	William Lane	40,000
1595	James Lancaster	50,000
1607	John Ward	100,000

This chart shows some of the riches taken by English pirates from 1579 to 1607.

Pirate Flags

Pirate flags were used to strike fear into the hearts of sailors on honest ships. The first flags were blood red. These flags were raised by pirates before they entered into battle. They warned the crew on the other ship that no lives would be spared if they did not surrender.

Jack Rackam

Pirate flags often had a skull and crossbones on them. Many had swords, and skeletons on them. Most of the flags had either black or red backgrounds. The flags were known as the Jolly Roger.

The names under these flags show which pirates flew them.

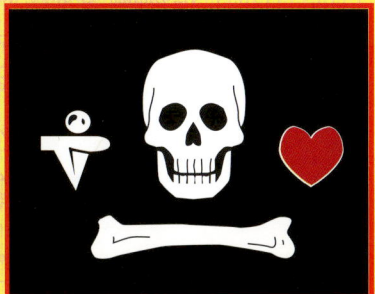

Stede Bonnet

Emanuel Wynne

Thomas Tew

Henry Every

A Pirate Attack

Pirates would attack any ship. They threw large grappling hooks attached to ropes onto the other ship. They then pulled the ships close together and jumped aboard, waving swords and firing their pistols.

Pirates were fierce fighters and they were mean. They would swing their swords, fire their pistols, stab with daggers, kick, punch, and even bite.

Pirates also carried muskets, which they packed with gunpowder and small lead balls. When they pulled the trigger, a spark set the gunpowder on fire. The exploding gunpowder sent the lead ball speeding to its target.

Pirates often killed the crew or threw them overboard, then took whatever they wanted. Sometimes they stole the ship, too. Ships that had no value to the pirates were usually sunk. Members of a ship's crew that were not killed might be forced to join the pirate crew.

Pirates of the Caribbean

One area that had more than its share of pirates was the Caribbean Sea. The map shows that the Caribbean is off the south-east coast of the United States.

After the Americas were discovered, ships laden with gold, furs, spices, and other riches often sailed through the Caribbean from the Americas to Europe. The ships' cargo made them heavy and slow. These ships became easy victims for pirates.

In the Caribbean there are many islands with coves where pirates could hide and wait to attack the ships.

There were pirates in many other parts of the world, particularly in the South China Sea where there are also many islands. But the pirates of the Caribbean were some of the best known because of their fierce and daring attacks.

Caribbean

Famous Pirates

Although pirates roamed the seas for more than 2,000 years, some of the most famous pirates were active during the Golden Age of Piracy. This was at the end of the seventeenth century and the beginning of the eighteenth century.

People today are interested in famous pirates and their ships. Sometimes people build life-sized models of pirates ships. This is a life-sized model of the Golden Hind.

Anne Bonny

Anne Bonny grew up disguised as a boy. When she was 16, she ran off to join a pirate crew.

Anne Bonny was a fierce fighter and one of the most famous of all the female pirates. She was captured in 1721 and sentenced to death, but she was allowed to go free when it was found that she was pregnant.

Anne Bonny was one of the most famous female pirates.

Blackbeard (Edward Teach)

Blackbeard was one of the most feared pirates of all time. He was born in England around 1680.

Blackbeard was a big man with a long black beard. Before an attack, he would tie fuses in his beard and light them. He boarded ships shouting loudly, with a sword in one hand, a pistol in the other, and his beard smoking from the fuses.

People were so scared of Blackbeard that they often surrendered without a fight.

Blackbeard was one of the most feared pirates ever.

Blackbeard died in a fierce battle against Lieutenant Maynard. Lieutenant Maynard had been sent by the Governor of Virginia to capture Blackbeard.

It took several pistol shots and about 20 stab wounds to kill Blackbeard. His head was cut off, and Maynard hung it on the front of his ship as a warning to other pirates.

Blackbeard was shot, and stabbed many times before he died.

Sir Francis Drake

An Englishman, Sir Francis Drake, was a well-known explorer. In the late 1500s he became a privateer. He led many attacks on Spanish ships that were carrying rich cargoes of gold.

He was made a knight by Queen Elizabeth I of England. She called Drake *my pirate*.

Queen Elizabeth made Sir Francis Drake a knight.

Captain William Kidd

Captain William Kidd was a privateer for the English government, but soon turned to piracy, probably for the money.

Captain William Kidd was quick tempered. He once threw a bucket at a crew member who said something that made him mad. The bucket hit the man on the head and killed him.

Captain William Kidd was a quick tempered man.

Kidd became very rich, but was eventually caught and hanged. His body was left hanging for a long time to discourage others from becoming pirates.

Kidd became very rich.

Interesting Pirate Stories

Pirating was a dangerous job. Pirates risked life and limb to capture the riches from another ship. To encourage their crews to enter into battle, pirate captains paid extra money to a pirate who was injured while fighting. If a pirate was blinded in one eye or lost a finger, he might get one hundred or more extra gold coins. If a leg or arm was lost, he would get even more.

Life aboard pirate ships was harsh. The pirates lived in crowded spaces and the food they ate was often stale rotten bread and salted meat. There was very little medicine to treat illness. The pirates often suffered from a disease called scurvy. They got scurvy when there were not enough fruit and vegetables to eat to provide Vitamin C to keep them healthy.

A pirate ship in the Caribbean once attacked and boarded a ship filled with valuable goods, including cocoa beans. The pirates thought the beans were sheep droppings and threw them all overboard.

Piracy was stopped by governments who wanted to have free trade and safe shipping in all seas.

Glossary

cannons – Large guns used in war.

cargo(es) – Goods carried in large quantities by a ship, plane, or truck.

colonies – Countries or areas ruled by a foreign country.

coves – Small, sheltered bays.

crew – A group of people working together on a vehicle, like a ship, train, or plane to keep it running smoothly.

grappling hooks – Iron hooks attached to a rope and used for grasping and dragging.

peace treaties – Agreements made between countries at war that there will be no more fighting.

pounds sterling – Basic monetary unit of the United Kingdom.

riches – Valuable goods and natural resources.